Love Notes

From

God

By: Dr. Ruth M Wilson

BK Royston Publishing

Jeffersonville, IN

BK Royston Publishing
P. O. Box 4321
Jeffersonville, IN 47131
502-802-5385
http://bkroystonpublishing.com
bkroystonpublishing@gmail.com

Cover DESIGNER: TED DONES
TLD GRAPHIC DESIGN
417.396.8295 | P.O.BOX 43881
LOUISVILLE, KY 40243
WWW.MESSENGERSOFFIRE.ORG

ISBN-13: 978-0692680971
ISBN-10: 0692680977

Printed in the United States of America

More Books by Dr. Ruth M. Wilson

Best Friends

Do You Have It?

Fully Equipped

How to Properly Talk to God

Purpose in the Midst of the Madness

Let us know, tell someone else, or if you would like to order additional copies send all correspondence to:

Dr. Ruth Wilson

P. O. Box 133

Louisville, KY 40201

Email us at: dauparoom@yahoo.com

Love Notes

From

God

Beloved

God

(Greatly loved)

I love you!

God

Behold, what manner of love the Father hath bestowed upon us, that we should be called the sons of God: therefore the world knoweth us not, because it knew him not.   1 John 3:1

I woke you up this morning!

God

Arise, shine; for thy light is come, and the glory of the LORD is risen upon thee. Isaiah 60:1

Remember to pray and thank me.

God

Be careful for nothing; but in every thing by prayer and supplication with thanksgiving let your requests be made known unto God. Philippians 4:6

Remember who you are.

God

But ye are a chosen generation, a royal priesthood, an holy nation, a peculiar people; that ye should shew forth the praises of him who hath called you out of darkness into his marvellous light; 1 Peter 2:9

For we are his workmanship, created in Christ Jesus unto good works, which God hath before ordained that we should walk in them.   Ephesians 2:10

Remember to speak life today.

God

Death and life are in the power of the tongue: and they that love it shall eat the fruit thereof. Proverbs 18:21

Remember to ask me for wisdom so you can make the right decisions and choices.

God

If any of you lack wisdom, let him ask of God, that giveth to all men liberally, and upbraideth not; and it shall be given him.   James 1:5

Remember I am your consultant.

God

"Trust in the LORD with all thine heart; and lean not unto thine own understanding. In all thy ways acknowledge him, and he shall direct thy paths."
Proverbs 3:5-6

You don't have to be fearful of anything or anybody

God

For God hath not given us the spirit of fear; but of power, and of love, and of a sound mind. 2 Timothy 1:7

Remember I'm always with you.

Qod

I will never leave thee, nor forsake thee. Hebrews 13:5

Remember you are powerful.

Got

Behold, I give unto you power to tread on serpents and scorpions, and over all the power of the enemy: and nothing shall by any means hurt you. Luke 10:19

Remember you can do anything you set your heart to do today

God

I can do all things through Christ which strengtheneth me. Philippians 4:13

Be watchful!

God

Be sober, be vigilant; because your adversary the devil, as a roaring lion, walketh about, seeking whom he may devour: 1 Peter 5:8

Remember everything will work in your favor

God

And we know that all things work together for good to them that love God, to them who are the called according to his purpose.   Romans 8:28

Remember to walk in love

God

and whatever you do, do it with kindness and love.
1Corinthians 16:14 Living Bible Version

Remember to do everything in a spirit of excellence.

God

Let all things be done decently and in order.
1 Corinthians 14:40

Have a wonderful day.

God

This is the day which the Lord hath made; we will rejoice and be glad in it. *Psalm 118:24*

About the Author

Dr. Ruth M. Wilson is the Pastor and Founder of the Shekinah Glory International Ministries located in Louisville, KY.

Dr. Wilson is available to speak at workshops, conferences, revivals, all media interviews and can be contacted via the information below.

Let us know, tell someone else or if you would like to order additional copies send all correspondence to:

Dr. Ruth Wilson

P. O. Box 133

Louisville, KY 40201

Email us at: dauparoom@yahoo.com